FIRESIDE CHAT

Jack Mitchell

Scriptural quotes from *The Holy Bible*, New International Version, Zondervan Publishing House, 1995; *The Holy Bible,* Ignatius Press, 2006; *The Holy Bible*, New King James Version, Thomas Nelson, Inc., 1982.

Printed in the United States of America.

ISBN-13: 978-1466400764

ISBN-10: 1466400765

Cover design: Jim Morrill

"Now war arose in heaven, Michael and his angels fighting against the dragon; and the dragon and his angels fought, but they were defeated and there was no longer any place for them in heaven. And the great dragon was thrown down, that ancient serpent, who is called the Devil and Satan, the deceiver of the whole world—he was thrown down to the earth, and his angels were thrown down with him."

—Rev. 12:7-9

GLORIA IN EXCELSIS DEO

For Natalia

Acknowledgements

Sincere thanks to my friends, David and Rhonda Thayer, for their invaluable assistance in typing the manuscript, with special thanks to Dave for asking all the right questions.

I'd also like to thank my old friend Jim Morrill for his help with the editing process and in formatting the book for publication.

Jack Mitchell

October 2011

NOTE TO READER

I decided to write this book, which is based on several conversations with my friend David Thayer, using an interview style for two reasons: I thought it would make it easier for the reader to digest, and I really like communicating important concepts by way of dialogue.

I hope the reader agrees.

—*Jack Mitchell*

CONTENTS

Chapter One

THE FUNDAMENTAL OPTION

"I have set before you life and death, blessing and

cursing; therefore choose life."

—Deuteronomy 30:19

Jack: A few years ago, I was diagnosed with non-Hodgkin's lymphoma. The news came as a complete shock, since I've always been a healthy guy: Very athletic, never smoked, good diet, etc. The call really took my breath away; instantly, everything seemed to slow way down. I became acutely aware of the smallest things, all the "stuff" of life that one takes for granted; I remember staring out across the lake at a pair of ducks for the longest time.

That afternoon I recalled an old Spanish proverb, that when a man suddenly finds himself caught between the sword and the wall, it concentrates his mind wonderfully. *For sure.*

When the sun began to set that evening I asked myself this: If I had known that this was to be my last day, how would I have chosen to live it? It's a question worth asking.

Among other things, I realized that *everything* depends upon the individual choices we make, especially the disposition of our eternal soul.

Nothing is "mundane": When we hold a door open for a stranger, let someone ahead of us in traffic, or give a sincere compliment to an overworked store clerk. Whatever we choose to do, or not do, whatever we choose to say, or not say, may have consequences that exceed our immediate comprehension.

For instance, one night when I was working as a corrections officer in a county jail, an inmate asked to speak with me privately. With intense emotion, he told me that he had been planning to commit suicide, until he overheard me talking one evening to a group of inmates in his section. He had listened as I spoke of life as a precious gift, of God's love for each of us in a unique and personal way (no exceptions), and that it was possible to be healed of the wounds of a lifetime. That very night this man chose to live; he literally chose life over death.

In reflecting back on this incident I had a renewed appreciation of the effect our words and actions can have on those around us. How we choose to live our lives matters more than we know; like it or not, we truly are our brother's keeper.

Dave: I never thought of it that way. It's really about taking personal responsibility, isn't it?

Jack: Yes.

Dave: Tell me, what is "the fundamental option"?

Jack: The fundamental option is a theological term that refers to the one critical choice that confronts us all, on a daily basis; a decision of the will that cannot be evaded or ignored. Simply stated, we're presented with a choice between two gods; we must decide for ourselves which one to worship and serve.

The first lives right under our nose in the form of an unconverted ego, willfully determined to celebrate the wonder of itself—no matter the cost—without a shred of humility or concern for the needs of others. When we routinely choose self-exaltation as the primary expression of our existence, we are soon joined at the hip by the serpent of old; together, we begin the long, slow dance of death into the place of endless darkness.

Our second option is the Lord God of Hosts, in the person of Jesus Christ, who is the Light of the World. He told us: "I am the Resurrection and the Life. He who believes in Me will live, even though he dies; and whoever lives and believes in

Me will never die. Do you believe this?" —John
11:25, 26

"*Do you believe this?*" That is the ultimate
question, isn't it? In fact, this is really the only
question that matters in the end. But what about
right now?

> "*...I do believe; help me overcome my unbelief!*"
>
> —Mark 9:24

For many people today the public expression of an actual belief in a personal God has
become little more than a pro forma nod to a
pleasant childhood myth; it contains about the
same degree of religious conviction evoked by "In
God We Trust" on our folding money. At best,
God is generally regarded as a sort of benevolent

police officer up in the sky (who bears a striking resemblance to the late Charlton Heston). Far removed from the gritty details of our lives, He assumes a posture of benign indifference, except, of course, when we do something wrong. Then: *Wham!*

This widely-held perception may explain why a polled majority of Americans are bored out of their minds during church services, and why so many others have opted out altogether. And from their perspective, who can blame them? "Going to church" seems like a waste of time (and money); they're like fish swimming around in the ocean in an endless search for water. Discouraged and exhausted, they eventually tell themselves, and others: "It's no use; I've looked for water everywhere; it just doesn't exist. Time to move on."

Commenting on the human condition in the 16th century, St. Theresa of Avila said that most of our problems are indeed caused by a lack of belief that God is truly present to us.

Agreed. But how do we "get" the awareness of His presence? How does God become real to us?

One irrefutable fact of life is that whatever we choose to focus on inevitably manifests itself in our experience, either positively or negatively.

Why not focus on God?

God yearns for our friendship, but not wanting to impose on our free will, waits for us to make the opening move. Blessedly, when we take our first timid step toward Him, He takes a thousand steps toward us.

From our perspective this is called "prayer", and at the heart of all prayer is the desire for union with God. Consciously or unconsciously, all of creation (with a few notable exceptions) is inclined to turn in the direction of its Creator. As God is in a unique relationship with each of us, this "turning" can take many forms.

In my own case I've found "The Jesus Prayer" (from the Eastern Orthodox tradition) to be most helpful in "making contact" with the realized presence of God on a daily basis. This simple prayer, "Lord Jesus Christ, Son of God, have mercy on me", when repeated silently and in rhythm with the breath (for about 20 minutes twice a day, morning and evening), leads the soul into a deeper and deeper awareness of its oneness with God. A feeling of warmth is often felt throughout the body, which affirms the actual presence of the Holy Spirit. Some prefer to simply repeat the sacred name of "Jesus", using the same method. Either way is fine; just do it!

I also recommend the timeless spiritual classic, *The Practice of the Presence of God*, a book of conversations and letters by Nicholas Herman of Lorraine, better known as Brother Lawrence. I found this little book several years before discovering "The Jesus Prayer". The book, written by a humble monk in the 17th century, has never been out of print, and has had a profound impact on my spiritual life. Brother Lawrence taught that if we truly desire a closer walk with God, we must take some time each day to be as consciously present to Him, as He is to us.

> *"You have made known to me the ways of life;*
> *you will make me full of gladness with your presence."*
> —Acts 2:28

Together, *The Practice of the Presence of God* and "The Jesus Prayer" are deeply transformational, and can bring God to life in the heart of any frustrated Christian and even, perhaps, the most reluctant agnostic.

> *"I have loved you with an everlasting love."*
> —Jeremiah 31:3
> *"I have called you by name; you are Mine."*
> —Isaiah 43:1

Dave: Thanks Jack, that was great. Any final thoughts before we close for today?

Jack: Today's topic, "the fundamental option", brings to mind a favorite parable:

Once upon a time, a man was forced to leave the safety and security of his homeland. Lonely and afraid, he had walked for many miles, when he suddenly came to the lip of a steep canyon; startled, he jumped back just in time. Shaking with fear, he took a deep breath, and then looked around; he quickly realized there was no way for him to get across the immense chasm; the bottom was so far down he couldn't even see it.

Then he looked up again. To his surprise, he saw a man standing on the other side, dressed as an acrobat, smiling at him. Not only that, the man was holding the handles of a wheelbarrow, which he then proceeded to push ahead of him on a single wire that stretched across the abyss.

The acrobat skillfully made his way over to the traveler, stepped off, and said: "Hello friend … what'd you think of that?"

The traveler was completely astonished; he had never seen anything like this, and told the acrobat so.

Then the acrobat asked him: "Do you think I could do it again?" The man paused for a moment, and then answered with enthusiasm: "Of course! I absolutely believe you could do it again!"

"Good!" said the acrobat. "Get in the wheelbarrow and I'll take you across!"

Ah … The moment of truth. Will you get in the wheelbarrow? *Or not?*

The decision is yours, and yours alone.

Chapter Two

THE PRINCE OF DARKNESS

"Evil is not merely a lack of something, but an effective agent, a living spiritual being, perverted and perverting. A terrible reality. Mysterious and frightening. It is contrary to the teaching of the Bible and the church to refuse to recognize the existence of such a reality, or to regard it as a principle in itself which does not draw its origin from God like every other creature; or to explain it as a pseudo-reality, a conceptual and fanciful personification of the unknown cause of our misfortunes."

—Pope Paul VI, Vatican General Audience

November 15, 1972

Dave: In our previous conversation you spoke on the subject of personal choice, and the importance of choosing well. What is your take on Lucifer's fundamental choice to reject God in favor of himself?

Jack: As informed by Christian theology and tradition we believe that God created an order of highly gifted, intelligent beings called "angels", who were free to love and serve Him in the everlasting magnificence of His creation; they were also free to reject Him. According to Scripture, Lucifer chose the latter course, for reasons that continue to elude us.

Was it pride? Jealousy? We really don't know. One thing is clear, however: Lucifer's decision to exalt himself over his Creator was the ultimate blasphemy, the primordial sin.

The result was his immediate expulsion from Paradise, along with all the angels who had sided with him.

> *"So the great dragon was cast out, that serpent of old, called the devil and Satan, who deceives the whole world; he was cast to the earth, and his angels were cast out with him."*
> —Rev. 12:9

Their banishment from the realized presence of God was eternal, precisely because it was irrevocable.

Dave: That's one thing that has always puzzled me. Why was God's judgment irrevocable?

Jack: Contrary to popular myth, God is neither capricious nor vindictive; quite the opposite. In His love for us He endowed both angelic spirits and humans with a reflective consciousness, i.e. the freedom to choose. God always defers to our choices, no matter how much those choices surely grieve Him at times; He couldn't do otherwise and still be God.

Unlike us, angels are solely comprised of intellect and will. Their preternatural intelligence and conscious awareness far exceeds ours—hence the choices they make are extremely well informed. The suicidal decision to reject God was carried out in spite of their complete, a priori knowledge of the seriousness and gravity of the offense, with full consent of the will, and total understanding of the inevitable consequence.

Lucifer's intended destiny was to love; defiant and unrepentant, he chose to be the source of endless hate instead. In expelling him from heaven God merely ratified this one terrible choice, for all eternity.

Dave: Though exiled from heaven, it's obvious that these fallen angels are not resting comfortably in some remote corner of the universe. The effects of their evil presence and power can be felt throughout the world. What can you tell us about the influence of evil spirit on our own disordered choices (sin)?

Jack: It is clear that Christianity would be incomprehensible if we refuse to acknowledge the reality of evil and its ruinous impact on individuals and society.

The tactics of the Evil One, especially regarding our moral choices, have not changed since the Adam and Eve event. "You will be like God" was his seductive lie to our first parents, which was a direct appeal to their pride and vanity. And they went for it.

All too often, so do we. Consider the interminable banalities of television commercials, enticing us with clever lies that promise perpetual youth and beauty, pain-free living, financial abundance and sexual fulfillment. And the subliminal message within this non-stop assault on our senses is: If you still have room on your credit card, who needs God?

The good news is that we are not alone and helpless:

> *"I have told you these things, so that in Me you may have peace. In this world you will have trouble. But take heart! I have overcome the world."*
>
> —John 16:33

And evil spirit, though powerful, is constrained by certain limitations imposed by God. As we have seen, it can assail us with temptations, even create conditions favorable to sin, but that's about it.

The media, especially movies and television, tend to portray demons as all-powerful, but that is simply not true. The devil and his operatives cannot "make" us do anything. As rational beings we always retain our free will, which is a gift from God, and cannot be abrogated by Satan. God does not permit this.

The final decision to violate our conscience, to commit an actual sin, has to come from within. We are quite capable of offending God all by ourselves, without any help from an external force. My years of work as a corrections officer persuaded me that most of our problems are self-generated, and that the first step in solving them usually involves the acceptance of personal responsibility.

However, I learned something else during my time in corrections that opened my eyes to another reality, one that I had not yet considered.

Dave: What was that?

Jack: Like most people I had always held a vague belief in the *existence* of evil; I had yet to encounter the living reality, the actual *presence* of evil. There is a profound difference, as I discovered late one night in the correctional facility.

Dave: What happened?

Jack: I was speaking with an inmate in a private conference room. This inmate was serving time for multiple offenses, including fraud by check and other forms of theft. He was also an alcoholic, but never violent. This guy was a smooth operator; his excuses and denials always contained a remarkable degree of plausibility. Most of the staff actually considered him a "model prisoner": He was cooperative, cheerful and seemed to get along well with other inmates. His disarming charm and sincere manner fooled nearly everyone; he always wore the same smiling mask.

But I began to sense something about this individual that made me feel uncomfortable; nothing tangible, no smoking gun as they say, just the hint of a threat lurking at the edge of my awareness. It made me wary because I couldn't identify it … not yet.

On the night in question I decided to confront him about some money that had been stolen from another inmate in his section. He smiled at me while denying any knowledge of the theft, even though I had presented him with proof of his guilt.

Then it happened. As I was about to send him back to his cell there was an abrupt shift in the atmosphere of the room; it was palpable. I became aware of another presence; we were no longer alone. As I turned toward the inmate I suddenly saw something in his eyes that hadn't been there the moment before, something bestial and predatory, glaring at me with such ferocious intensity that in the clarity of the moment I knew it wanted to kill me.

Taken aback, I said a silent prayer, asking God to reveal to me in a clear and definitive way exactly what I was dealing with: Was this man just another slick, garden-variety liar with an alcoholic addiction, or was there something else? Could this be a case of demonic possession?

I'll never forget what happened next: As the inmate and I continued to stare at each other, the room suddenly filled with the overwhelming stench of sulfur, which is the smell of hell *(Rev. 19:20)* and signifies the actual presence of demons. God had forced the enemy to reveal itself, to come out of the shadows, in answer to my prayer.

This dramatic event had a major impact on my life as a Christian. As a man who had come of age in an era of moral and spiritual relativism, in a media-driven culture dominated by cynicism and sneering contempt for traditional American values, of psycho-babble and situational ethics, I was stunned by the immediacy and shocking reality of the undeniable presence of evil.

This was my wake-up call; any lingering doubts about the existence of the devil had evaporated in an instant. Without knowing it at the time, I had found my vocation—rather, it had found me.

Dave: What did you do then?

Jack: For much of the next decade I studied the subject of evil, including its methodology and tactics, discernment of spirits, and the various means of deliverance from demonic infestation, oppression (demonization) and possession.

Over the years I've been privileged to assist a number of individuals who have experienced difficulty in this area, including members of the clergy. I mostly teach, but there are times when actual deliverance is necessary.

Unfortunately, far too many people are needlessly frustrated in their attempts to get spiritual help with these issues when they desperately need it. This is inexcusable.

When psychology became our de facto national religion many ministers and priests responded to those in crisis not with the power and authority imparted to them by Jesus of Nazareth, but by reflexively referring these tormented souls to "counseling" or to clinics where they could be medicated for their condition.

Often what was needed was deliverance from evil, in the name of Jesus Christ. Psychology has much to commend it, as do certain helpful medications, but psychology alone will never save us.

Dave: It seems that most professional people, including many theologians and clergy alike, no longer believe in the existence of the devil. What do you say to them?

Jack: I tell them that they have been deceived, and remind them of Charles Baudelaire's famous observation: "The greatest trick the devil ever played was convincing the world that he did not exist."

I also tell them, **reality is that which, even if you refuse to believe in it, doesn't go away**. Crudely stated, if you decide to jump off a 10-story building, you're free to deny the law of gravity all the way down, but the end result is always the same.

Look, I can only speak from personal experience: The devil is real. He is the great deceiver, the enemy of God and man, and is all about death: The death of joy, the death of hope, the death of love, and the death of soul.

Jesus called the devil "a murderer from the beginning" and "the father of lies" (*John 8:44*). The devil is the author of chaos, confusion, and disunity, and is the embodiment of living hate.

Many people today are prone to dismiss all this as a bunch of superstitious nonsense. For a long time now much of the Western world has rejected the possibility of a malevolent being who is at war with God in a cosmic struggle for the souls of men. It can be very difficult for people of good will to even contemplate the existence of such a dreadful reality.

Many would prefer to think of the devil as a rather dapper fellow, dressed in a silly red costume, who is mischievous in a hip sort of way, but largely ineffectual.

In fact, nothing could be further from the truth. In 1884 Léon Bloy wrote: "We may be assured that the devil of most of our poets would not frighten the youngest child ... But the real Satan, whom we no longer know ... he is so monstrous that if this slave were allowed to show himself as he is —in all the supernatural nakedness of non-love— the human race and the whole animal world would utter a cry of horror and fall dead."

The time for sophistry and wishful thinking is over. Hell is real; so is the devil.

† *The Prayer of Commitment* †

Do you renounce Satan and all wrongdoing?
Yes or No?

Do you believe that Jesus is the Son of God, that He died to free us from our sins, and that He rose to bring us new life? *Yes or No?*

Do you promise to follow Jesus as your Lord?
Yes or No?

Lord Jesus Christ, I want to belong to You from now on. I want to be free from the dominion of darkness and the rule of Satan, and I want to enter into Your kingdom and be a part of Your people. I will turn away from all wrongdoing and I will avoid everything that leads me to wrongdoing. I ask You to forgive all the sins that I have committed and I offer my life to You. I promise to listen to You and obey You as my Lord. I ask You to baptize me in the Holy Spirit and seal me with Your unconditional love.

Lord of my life, I surrender to You everything that I am, and all that I will be.   Amen.

Chapter Three

ALL DECEPTION, ALL THE TIME:
THE FATHER OF LIES AND THE AMERICAN LEFT

"Why do you not understand what I say? It is because you cannot bear to hear my word. You are of your father the devil, and your will is to do your father's desires. He was a murderer from the beginning and has nothing to do with the truth, because there is no truth in him. When he lies, he speaks according to his own nature, for he is a liar and the father of lies."

—John 8:43, 44

Dave: Jack, in our last conversation you mentioned coming of age in an era of moral and spiritual relativism. Would you care to comment on that?

Jack: Sure, but my answer won't be for the faint of heart; I'll give it to you straight. Evil spirit, settling over the land like a shroud of deadly ground fog, has slowly enveloped our nation in its suffocating grip. At long last, deceived and over-run by the forces of darkness, America is on the verge of collapsing like a house of cards.

This didn't happen overnight. The serpent can be very patient when eyeing his prey; he has all the time in the world.

Remember the story of the frog? If you put a frog into a pot of boiling water it immediately jumps out and runs away. But if you place the same frog into a container of room-temperature water it feels right at home and starts swimming around. As the temperature is gradually increased, the frog eventually dies, never realizing what has happened to it.

Like to us:

"Indeed the safest road to Hell is the gradual one—the gentle slope, soft underfoot, without sudden turnings, without milestones, without signposts."
—C.S. Lewis, *The Screwtape Letters*

Hypnotized and slowly led astray by the fairy tales and Alice-in-Wonderland nonsense of avant-garde "progressives" in the early 1960s, many Americans became increasingly disconnected from their core values. Unduly influenced by the godless media and emerging sub-culture of bohemian degenerates, and seduced by the siren call of materialism, scores of people found no greater purpose in life than the satisfaction of their individual desires.

Consequently, they became confused about basic moral issues of good and evil, right and wrong. "Truth" was tacitly redefined as a notional concept, expediently useful to the degree that random elasticity would permit, but otherwise ignored. And as more and more Americans walked away from the central organizing religious principles that had always sustained them, God was reduced to an abstract.

Stiff-armed by spiritual apathy, secular humanism, and a universal regression to pre-Christian levels of barbarity and depravity, God finally did the only thing He could do: He left us to ourselves.

"They have chosen their own ways,

and their souls delight in their abominations."

—Isaiah 66:3

As millions of people celebrated their new-found freedom from religion, the devil celebrated right along with them—but for a different reason. They belonged to him now.

This cultural apostasy, or the rejection of God, is what theologians refer to as "hell" in its most basic configuration.

Spiritually adrift and clueless, Americans were now more vulnerable than ever. The next assault on traditional morality and personal accountability came from the new kid on the block, "pop-psychology".

Promoted by airy-fairy types in academia, the media and liberal churches as a marvelous substitute for clear thinking and common sense, pop-psychology came equipped with its own baffling lexicon of ready-made excuses for the most egregious behaviors imaginable. As others have noted, our culture's rapid descent into decadence has been chiefly characterized by the virtual apotheosis of individual self-interest; even the most shocking forms of evil could now be rationalized and explained away by hordes of pin-headed gurus who couldn't even park their bicycles straight.

Unfortunately, when everything can be rationalized, then everything can be trivialized, including life itself. And real prices are paid.

For example, there have been well over 50 million abortions performed in the United States alone since 1973; a few years ago I met a woman who had had five and was contemplating a sixth. Think about that.

Dave: That's hard to imagine, Jack, even by today's standards.

Jack: Are you kidding? *What* standards? Dave, if it were possible to take a snapshot of an ordinary day in American life just a few short decades ago, and liken it to the culture today, it would blow your mind. The very same behaviors, language and dress that civilization long ago rejected as affronts to common decency have now gained wide acceptance. As a condition of our pseudo-sophistication we have allowed ourselves to be utterly saturated with the most unspeakable wickedness and depravity; Sodom and Gomorrah had nothing on 21st century America. The so-called "entertainment industry" has become a miasma of filth: As long ago as 1961 the then chairman of the Federal Communications Commission, Newton Minow, referred to television as "a vast wasteland". How quaint. I wonder what he would call it now?

Consider this: In the late Fall of 2010, the taxpayer-funded National Portrait Gallery, one of the museums of the Smithsonian Institution, showed a 4-minute homo-erotic video, "A Fire In My Belly", depicting images of an ant-covered Jesus, male genitalia, men in chains, the bloody mouth of a man being sewn shut, naked brothers kissing and more.

All this was on display during the Christmas season. Isn't that nice? Can you imagine bringing your children to visit the Smithsonian, for perhaps the first time, and having them exposed to this kind of garbage? How would you explain it to them? How *could* you explain it to them?

In response to the storm of criticism generated by this abomination, Smithsonian officials decided to remove the exhibit, a wise move. But why did they allow it in the first place?

By the way, the art critic of the *Washington Post*, one Blake Gopnik, was incensed by the museum's decision to pull the exhibit. How dare they, he demanded. After all, Gopnik had just given it a "rave review", declaring it was full of "wonderful art". This jackanape then imperiously proclaimed, "Common standards of decency should not exist in a pluralist society."

Really? Who knew?

Dave: What in the world has happened to us? This is insane.

Jack: Nothing "happened" to us, Dave. We did it to ourselves. It all started when the liberal U.S. Supreme Court, under Chief Justice Earl Warren, decided to remove any reference to God from American public school classrooms in 1962. That's when the wheels came off; our country has been in decline ever since.

A legalist to the core, Satan seized this opportunity to forge a permanent, symbiotic relationship with the American left, a relationship that has only grown stronger with the passage of time.

None of the devastating effects of this ungodly union has been more conspicuously vile than the destruction of modern American cities; these once vibrant centers of culture and commerce were turned into demon-infested pits by an avalanche of utopian social economic policies, designed to assuage liberal guilt under the guise of "compassion".

This demonic scam was perpetrated on a gullible American public by egalitarian leftists and greedy Democratic politicians who have been the sole purveyors of all this taxpayer-funded largesse, dating back to the Johnson Administration. Among other things, this socialist "Great Society" farce enabled corrupt lawmakers to create myriad clusters of self-perpetuating fiefdoms; in exchange for trillions of dollars squandered on endless boondoggle giveaway programs, they asked the serfs for only one thing in return: Their vote.

And it worked. In fact, it worked so well that the same politicians kept getting re-elected again and again and again. They found that by using class-warfare rhetoric to encourage a culture of dependency, victimization, and resentment towards "The Man", they could easily remain in power, and enjoy all the perks that came with it.

Unfortunately, in this brave new world of urban liberal hegemony and political correctness, traditional family structures disintegrated; drug dealers, poverty pimps, race hustlers, savage street criminals (and their naive enablers) and the sexual perversion lobby all flourished; the middle class fled. The beast was now in control.

But in keeping millions of people in perpetual bondage to a plantation mentality of dependency and hopelessness, while carefully redacting any mention of "personal responsibility" from their campaign speeches, these self-serving political hacks stole something from their constituents that could never be replaced: Their dignity, their self-respect, and, all too often, the quintessence of what it means to be human—their souls.

Yet, in typical Orwellian fashion, while striving to maintain a straight face, left-wing social engineers and Marxist professors continue to refer to this multi-generational travesty, this chronic national disgrace, in paradigmatic terms such as "social justice", "equality", and "freedom from oppression".

I call it something else: Hell on earth.

Make no mistake: The time for sugarcoating the threats to our nation's survival has expired. The stark reality is that Western Christian civilization is under direct assault from within by the forces of evil. We are engaged in deadly combat, as Jesus was, against an unholy, preternatural alliance of hissing serpents, who have emerged from the fetid, stygian bowels of the netherworld, all spawned by the same father—Satan.

Dave: I agree. Can you give an example of what we're dealing with?

Jack: Certainly. Do you remember the infamous photograph, "Piss Christ"? It was a depiction of the crucified Jesus submerged in a jar of the artist's own urine.

At first, people thought that this had either been found in a garbage dump, or left behind by a group of Satan worshippers. They were wrong.

In fact, this mockery of the Son of God, produced by some creature from hell named Andres Serrano in 1987, was an acclaimed "work of art", proudly displayed in galleries around the world. Not to be outdone, in 1989 the taxpayer-funded (of course) National Endowment for the Arts agreed to sponsor an exhibition of Serrano's "art" in this country, until the ensuing public outcry, led by Christian conservatives, forced them to reconsider.

The liberal reaction was predictably hysterical, screaming that this was an attack on "free speech". Free speech, indeed.

With a wink and a nod, and bowing to the god of political correctness, society has elevated the concept of "tolerance" to an absurdly new level; in lieu of traditional standards it is now considered a virtue to be "tolerant" of almost anything. Hooray! Free condoms for everyone! Piss Christ!

What lunacy.

Let me ask you something: Could these depraved assaults on the moral sensibilities of average American families really be what the Founding Fathers envisioned when they pledged "their lives, their fortunes, and their sacred honor" in the cause of freedom? Do you seriously think that these brave men would have chosen to suffer and die in places like Lexington, Valley Forge, and Saratoga if they had known what America would become, 200 years hence? And that if they voiced their objection to this smorgasbord of evil that they would be accused of "intolerance", "hate speech" or "homophobia"?

Can you imagine what their patriotic response would be? Probably something akin to: "Praise the Lord and pass the ammunition!"

Let us revisit "Piss Christ" for a moment: As the liberal elites were vehemently defending the public display of this gross obscenity, their equally loathsome peers were working feverishly to remove all traditional portrayals of the sacred everywhere else.

The American left's obsessive, anti-religious fervor is comparable to the relentlessly aggressive and painstakingly comprehensive suppression of religion in communist countries such as China, North Korea and the former Soviet Union. Take heed: If the left succeeds in fulfilling its godless agenda, especially through the liberal court system, our remaining religious freedoms will be lost forever.

Americans are much closer to experiencing this reality than they know.

Dave: These people are really dangerous.

Jack: Yes, they are, primarily because they are not really "people" in the ordinary sense;

there was an aberration in their genetic spiritual makeup, an empty space where the ontological presence of God should have been. Ever alert, and meeting with no resistance, evil spirit slithered into the vacuity of their soulless lives, which is why they all share the same reptilian conscious-ness. There is only one demon, but it has assumed many forms:

"Then Jesus asked him, 'What is your name?' 'My name is Legion,' he replied, 'for we are many.'"
—Mark 5:9

Thoughtful people can no longer afford the luxury of snoozing past the plethora of prattle, disingenuous rhetoric, and breathtaking lies ooz-ing forth from the masters of deceit in the Obama

White House. To engage these professional dissemblers in the foggy give-and-take of polite discourse is provably self-defeating, and is no substitute for speaking the plain truth, which is the only thing they fear.

Dave: What motivates these creatures?

Jack: When you manage to strip away their phony mask of benevolence you find they are motivated by the same misanthropic hatred of humanity that they inherited from their father the devil.

Dave: Can you cite a specific example?

Jack: Of course. Consider the evil of abortion, a horrendous sin against God and his creation: Abortion is state-sanctioned, premeditated murder, perpetrated under the fig-leaf disguise of the benign sounding approbation "choice", a satanic lie of such Hitlerian proportions that it would have been worthy of any Third Reich expert in propaganda or eugenics.

Babies do not "choose" to die; who consults them?

The selective compassion and transparent hypocrisy of "pro-choice" fundamentalists is astounding. The very same people who wouldn't dream of disturbing a nesting tern or a Tennessee River snail darter have no problem supporting the torture and dismemberment of a defenseless, unborn human baby. The people who promote and support such legalized infanticide are routinely referred to as "moderates" by the liberal culture;

those of us who stand against this shocking barba-rism are mocked as "extremists".

Speaking of Nazis, a few years ago I asked a hard-core Obama supporter (and strict vegetarian) how he could possibly justify the slaughter of mil-lions of innocents within their mothers' wombs.

"It's their karma," he shrugged.

"Really?" I asked. "So how do you explain the Jewish holocaust? Was this their 'karma' also?"

"Of course," he replied. "Nothing and no one dies without giving their permission, at some level, including the Jews and all those babies you're so upset about."

End of conversation.

Dave: What evil. What else are these people trying to accomplish?

Jack: If one has the stomach for it, and can sift through multiple layers of corruption, distortion, and shameless dishonesty, it becomes increasingly clear that these creatures have coalesced their energies and considerable resources around one core objective: They want to destroy us, and our way of life.

They want to destroy our economic system, our educational system, our history, our Judeo-Christian foundation and our Constitution. Many of them, <u>including Barack Obama</u>, regard the United States Constitution as an impediment, a relic from the past, a nuisance to be either ignored or circumvented, except when it can be used or successfully perverted for the sake of political and or social expediency.

The effectiveness of these seemingly disparate, albeit politically incestuous groups to wreck our country and re-shape it in accord with their own diabolic fantasies is largely dependent upon the philosophical and practical support given them by their amoral allies in the media, politics, academia and the "arts".

> *"Their throats are open graves; their tongues practice deceit … And there is no fear of God before their eyes."*
> —Romans 3:13, 18

I'm constantly amazed by the rivers of effluence that flow from the mouths of liberal politicians and their sycophantic media spin-doctors; it's all deception, all the time.

These "opinion makers" are experts in manipulating the public perception of reality; what makes them especially dangerous is that they have no self-regulating mechanism of either conscience or principle. They know it's possible for an entire nation to be deceived, because it's been done before. Joseph Goebbels, key architect of the Nazi propaganda machine, said that if you repeat the same lie often enough, it eventually becomes the truth. He would know.

The nabobs in the mainstream media have been using this technique for over 50 years now, with great success. Satan is delighted to co-opt these unprincipled jackals, of course, along with the leaders and methodologies of other left-wing fraternities, such as the A.C.L.U., as their goals so frequently coincide with his own. These odious people, laughingly referred to by Joseph Stalin as "useful idiots", have served Satan well, and done great harm to our republic.

But here's the kicker: All that I've been de-scribing, including the Kafkaesque absurdities of the radical left, is nothing but a giant shell game, orchestrated by the Father of Lies himself.

Watch the other hand: *The real war for America's soul is spiritual, not political.*

Aeschylus noted that in war, truth is the first casualty. In spiritual warfare, politics is just a smokescreen, an elaborate diversion; if we fall for it, and allow ourselves to be overly distracted by the passions and personalities of the moment, we are bound to overlook the one who stands behind the curtain—directing all their moves.

In his letter to the people of Ephesus, Paul clearly identified the real enemy:

"Put on the full armor of God, so that you can take your stand against the devil's schemes. For we wrestle not against flesh and blood, but against principalities,

> *against powers, against the rulers of the darkness of this present age, against spiritual hosts of wickedness in high places."*
> —Ephesians 6:11,12

Dave: Wow. I feel like I've been run over by a truck —can we take a break?

Jack: You bet. See you tomorrow.

Chapter Four

THE HUSTLER

*"A horrible and shocking thing has happened in the land: The prophets prophesy falsely ... **And my people love to have it so.**"*
—Jeremiah 5:30, 31

*"You can fool some of the people all of the time,
and all of the people some of the time,
but you cannot fool all the people all of the time."*
—Abraham Lincoln

Dave: Although Barack Obama's layers of deception cling to him like filthy rags, many people continue to embrace him. Why?

Jack: Because they can't handle the truth. Like the deluded devotees of other cult figures, they are so emotionally invested in their illusions they refuse to see that their "hero" is leading them right over a cliff. They are totally deceived, and clueless.

> *" … the God of this world*
> *has blinded the minds of the unbelievers … "*
> —II Corinthians 4:4

The election of Barack Hussein Obama as President of the United States was a shameful thing. People take on the characteristics of what-ever it is they swim in; marinated in a culture of liberal orthodoxy and spiritual indifference for decades, Americans were prime for seduction by a charming socialist demagogue like Barack Obama. The fact that the spirit of deception was all over him, and that he was totally unqualified to be president, seemed not to matter.

Obama quickly became the apogee of the progressive liberal cause; he was to be the fulfill-ment of every left-wing fantasy of the last 100 years. All their dreams and schemes were about to come true.

It hasn't happened. The American people, <u>many of whom had been stuck on stupid for at least two generations</u>, finally awakened from their media-induced coma. They came to realize that the Obama Administration is a cesspool of lies; lying comes naturally to them, like breathing. Obama is charismatic and quick on his feet, as were the Machiavellian Clintons before him; all three share the same uncanny, preternatural cleverness that enables them to survive the occasional, unscripted encounter with truth.

But Obama has something else in common with the Clintons, which may be the most telling trait of all: *No shame.* His official title "Commander-in-Chief" is a pathetic joke to most veterans, such as myself, and seasoned military professionals. Why? As a retired senior military intelligence officer explained to me last year, "If this character was a civilian he wouldn't qualify for even a low-level security pass at any United States military installation; his personal associations, past and present, with anti-American radicals and known domestic terrorists, in addition to a history of espousing left-wing socialist ideology, would automatically disqualify him from any serious consideration."

Obama's college indoctrination under the tutelage of socialist and Marxist professors, and part-time "work" as a "community organizer" in Chicago in no way prepared him for the most powerful executive position in the world. In fact, he had had no prior executive experience at all. None, whatsoever. Our self-avowed enemies are well aware of all this, of course, which makes us even more vulnerable to them.

This is certainly not the time for amateurs, but that's exactly what we've got in the current White House. In the midst of deadly conflagrations in the Middle East, existential threats to Israel, destabilization of Western European democracies, rising oil prices, the devaluation of our currency, an unsustainable national debt, a depressed housing market, an unemployment rate at nearly 10 percent, union-led riots in the heartland, urban "flash mobs", a massive tide of illegal immigration, earthquakes, tsunamis, historic floods, devastating tornadoes, and two wars, our "president" (last week) chose to focus his attention on … the status of homosexuals in the military! Give me a break—is it any wonder that our enemies laugh at us, and our allies no longer trust us?

The wolves are circling, and Obama has opened the gates. If self-preservation is the first law of nature, you ask, what is this farrago of nonsense all about? Why is the President of the United States acting so stupidly?

Answer: There is nothing stupid about Barack Obama; he's an expert in what circus hustlers call "misdirection". This guy may be a con man, all smoke and mirrors, but to write him off as clueless or incompetent is a serious miscalculation and plays right into the hands of the godless left; the inability of the American public to comprehend his underlying agenda does not make *him* confused. "Barry" knows exactly what he's doing; he and his minions are right on schedule.

None of what we've been witnessing can be considered "spontaneous events"—they are the result of years of careful and deliberate planning by the forces of evil. The left's diabolic stratagems for the systematic dismantling of our republic were outlined decades ago by liberal socialists and communist intellectuals. They waited a long time for someone like Barack Obama to grab the brass ring; in 2008 they hit the jackpot. Their moment had finally arrived, and they quickly got to work.

These people mean business. Consider the recent events in Madison, Wisconsin, and what is currently happening on Wall Street and in numerous other cities around the country. Given faux legitimacy by their counterculture friends in the liberal mainstream media, while chanting "death to capitalism" and urinating on police cars, a motley coalition of incoherent malcontents ("What do we want? We don't know! When do we want it? Now!") are staging a series of seemingly inchoate temper tantrums across America that are, in fact, deliberately designed to foment violence, intimidation, and instability; i.e. <u>revolution</u>. A churlish mobocracy of would-be anarchists, consisting of spoiled, directionless college kids, wild-eyed leftists, gray-haired hippies, labor union thugs, and the usual contingent of dopey Hollywood celebrities are all marching in lockstep, like submissive stooges, to the drumbeat reprise of Marxist revolutionary rhetoric. This is all part of a calculated, premeditated plan of action, <u>orchestrated by Democratic Party operatives and their wealthy backers</u>, who are in daily consultation with the Obama White House.

Karl Marx stated, "My object in life is to dethrone God and destroy capitalism." <u>Sound familiar</u>?

It's worth noting that any number of these very same "agents of change" are working under the radar in other countries as well. "A crisis is a terrible thing to waste" was the cynical strategic advice given them by Obama's former chief of staff, who is now the mayor of Chicago. Duly inspired, a committed cadre of uber-left subversives travel back and forth to Europe and the Middle East, either manufacturing said crises or exploiting situations that already look promising. Their intention, of course, is to create as much political, economic and social chaos as possible. <u>It doesn't matter what the issue is, as long as they can use it to achieve their objective.</u>

Dave: What *is* their objective?

Jack: Their revolutionary goal is to create a "new world order" by seizing power and control on an unprecedented, global scale. This is all unfolding right before our eyes, in dramatic fashion.

Dave: Can you give us a basic overview of their actual ground operation?

Jack: Sure. Their tactics seldom vary. The immediate objective in any targeted situation is to gain control of the media, then publicly identify a suitable scapegoat for the peoples' real or imagined frustrations, as Hitler did to the Jews in the 1930s, **and as Obama is attempting to do now**.

The next step is to whip the masses into a frenzy of sustained anger and rage, then fade back into the shadows, and let nature take its course. After the dust has settled they re-emerge, in perfect position to assume power and control.

Dave: How can they be confident of being on the winning side?

Jack: Because they understand something very basic about human nature. **They know that in the end, historically, people will always choose order over chaos, even if it means sacrificing their own liberty**. This is the secret of any successful political or military coup; it works every time.

Dave: It's really amazing how much can be accomplished by a determined group of people who have no conscience.

Jack: Precisely. Driven by a lust for power, and unencumbered by morality or ethics, these predators are capable of anything. To wit: In any artificially created crisis, a "strongman" will suddenly appear; he is well-spoken, has a sense of presence, and smiles a lot. With the aid of a servile media, and flanked by a few handpicked generals, he promises peace, stability, and a return to good times. All the people cheer, and some even weep for joy; their savior has arrived—and just in time.

Soon, their charming, newly-minted messiah shocks them into submission by declaring martial law (for their own good), abolishing the constitution, and ceding all political power to himself and his behind-the-scenes cronies, who helped him engineer the whole thing in the first place.

Don't think it could happen here? Think again; the world has seen this movie before. Germany was no banana republic either—remember?

> **"Those who ignore the past**
> **are condemned to repeat it."**
> **— George Santayana**

Enter Barack Hussein Obama:

Anointed by Satan's amen corner in the mainstream media as "the messiah", an obscure socialist radical from Chicago suddenly found himself walking around as the most powerful man on the planet.

Unrestrained by the normal self-governing limits of modesty and principle, this callow fraud announced his intention to *"fundamentally trans-form America"*, and he meant it. Once elected, he tried to do just that.

But his patina of charm and cunning intelligence eventually wore thin; the public's enthusiasm waned as more and more Americans saw through his smirking cleverness, class-warfare demagoguery, and bold-faced lies; in short, his kabuki theatre charades were no longer enough to insulate him from the hard lens of truth.

Unmasked, Barack Obama has been re-vealed as a poseur, an anti-Christian, anticapitalist, smooth-as-silk left-wing globalist with an under-developed conscience, driven by personal arrogance and political ambitions that may far exceed the parochial confines of 1600 Pennsylvania Avenue. This is a dangerous man.

It is clear that our constitutional republic is facing a serious existential threat from within; anyone with even a modicum of interest in the Book of Revelation should sit up and take notice.

"The great masses of the people ... will more easily fall victims to a big lie than to a small one."
— Adolf Hitler, *Mein Kampf I, 10*

Chapter Five

DELIVER US FROM EVIL

"What do you want with us, Jesus of Nazareth?

Have you come to destroy us?

I know who you are — the Holy One of God!"

—Mark 1:24

Dave: Let's talk about the subject of evil. How do you want to begin?

Jack: Evil is a complicated subject; by its very nature it is dark and disturbing. Most people avoid the topic altogether, if they can. But sometimes they can't. In fact, it's becoming increasingly difficult for any of us to ignore the presence of evil; we see evidence of the diabolic all around us.

Before we get too deep in the weeds, Dave, I'd like to offer a word of caution: Bear in mind that ignorance breeds fear, and fear breeds hostility, especially with regard to religion. In varying degrees what people are prone to call "evil" in others is often a projection of their own unintegrated darkness. Scapegoating is a convenient way to avoid looking within; before sallying forth with pitchforks and torches in the direction of some hapless apostate it would be wise to take our own inventory first.

The term "possession" is overused and little understood. Actual demonic possession, meaning the total abdication and yielding of intellect and will to an invading malevolent force, is a rare occurrence.

On the other hand, demonic infestation and oppression (I prefer the term "demonization") is quite common, and needs to be dealt with.

Dave: What's the difference between the two?

Jack: "Infestation" refers to diabolic possession of homes, businesses, animals, geographic areas and certain objects, especially those that have been used in occult rituals. "Poltergeist activity" is synonymous with demonic infestation, and is often characterized by strange noises, objects that move by themselves, foul odors, the tearing of wallpaper, sharp rapping sounds, freezing cold, ghostly apparitions and the like. These strange occurrences can be quite annoying, even frightening at times, but are generally harmless.

"Demonization", however, is quite different. This term is used to describe the spiritual condition that can befall an individual as a result of repeated demonic assaults on their senses, intellect and will. This is sometimes referred to as "the process of possession". Our de-Christianized society is rife with examples of this ongoing phenomenon.

The characteristics of demonization vary according to particular circumstances, but there is always one unmistakable sign: A peculiar, visceral aversion to sacred objects (such as a crucifix), and places and people who are closely associated with God. This indicates a condition of significant spiritual darkness, and, if left unchecked, may lead to complete demonic possession. It can't be ignored.

A few years ago I was called to a home here in New England that had been infested with demons for some 30 years, according to several corroborating witnesses: Ghostly apparitions, the stench of sulfur, weird noises, an unseen nightly visitor that jumped up and down on beds, and a low, threatening voice that commanded the owner to "leave".

At the family's request I blessed their home, going room to room, saying prayers of deliverance in the name of Jesus Christ. When I had finished, I sat down with them and offered the following suggestions: After a home has been swept clean of demons the family needs to discourage their return by establishing a God-centered environment. First, I recommended leaving their home Bible open to St. Paul's letter to the Philippians, Chapter two, verses 5-11:

Your attitude should be the same as that of Christ Jesus: Who, being in very nature God, did not consider equality with God something to be grasped, but made himself nothing, taking the very nature of a servant, being made in human likeness. And being found in appearance as a man, he humbled himself and became obedient unto death—even death on a cross!

Therefore God exalted him to the highest place and gave him the Name which is above every name, before which every knee shall bend, of those in heaven, of those on earth, and of those under the earth, and every tongue confess that Jesus Christ is Lord, to the glory of God the Father.

This particular passage speaks to the humility of Christ, but also to His divine majesty and power, which is why the devil and his gang of demons is repelled by it.

Remember, every possessing spirit, indeed every demon from hell, is terrified of the sacred name of "Jesus". They must obey any command, any adjuration spoken in the power of that Name.

Next, I talked about the value of individual and communal prayer, and how important it is for families to take the time to pray together, as often as possible. The Bible should take center stage in every Christian home, of course, but it shouldn't be collecting dust; there is simply no substitute for daily reading of the Word. Prayer time should also include some form of praise music, which evil spirit cannot stand.

Finally, I spoke about the power of love; when a family chooses the fundamental option to love, God is truly present to them (*I John 4:12,16*) and the devil flees. Why? Because evil spirit cannot comprehend love; it is antithetical to its nature and it has no defense against it. Creating an atmosphere of love is a family's most effective antidote to the would-be presence of evil; it actually sanctifies the home.

The deliverance was successful; there has not been a recurrence of any demonic activity for over five years, praise God.

Dave: How important is it for the victims of infestation or demonization to cooperate in their own healing and deliverance?

Jack: It's critical. Without the willful cooperation of the afflicted person(s), any effort on my part is usually futile. I've tried it; it just doesn't work.

Dave: Once again we return to the theme of personal responsibility.

Jack: There's no avoiding it. There is no such thing as "collective salvation". That was just another disingenuous thought-bubble dreamt up by the Obama Administration, in an attempt to put a religious spin on its corrupt socialist agenda. It didn't work.

Left-wing obfuscation aside, the fact is none of us has any greater responsibility in life than the obligation to care for our own individual soul. With that in mind, it is imperative that we acquire an awareness of and appreciation for basic spiritual truths early in life, which is essential for the proper formation of conscience and character. If this critical aspect of development has been neglected, for any reason, some may spend their entire lives in a spiritually unconscious state, unwittingly participating in their own downward spiral into the abyss.

Commenting on this condition, and our proclivity toward rationalization and spiritual sloth, the late theologian Martin Buber wrote of "the uncanny game of hide-and-seek, in the obscurity of the soul, in which it, the single human soul, evades itself, avoids itself, hides from itself."

Self-deception and cognitive dissonance are two sides of the same coin; arrogant ignorance can be just as deadly as intellectual pride. To remain blissfully unaware of the presence and tactics of the enemy is no defense against him; whistling past the graveyard only makes the devil smile, and won't save anyone.

Masses of people, including many nominal Christians, have foolishly allowed themselves to be led astray by all manner of counterfeit spirituality. To a person, they tend to regard the Bible as a fairy tale, a collection of tiresome myths written for the benefit of our unsophisticated ancestors, and totally irrelevant to life in the 21st century.

They much prefer to embrace their own shrewd insights and what passes for "wisdom" in the popular culture; many are loath to give up a spiritual philosophy or occult practice that makes them "feel good" or "isn't hurting anyone". Besides, they say, if all belief systems are relative, and therefore equally valid, *does it really matter what you believe*? A dash of this, a pinch of that, and pretty soon everything tastes the same.

Millions of Americans are in tacit agreement with this philosophy. It's called "syncretism", or the attempted reconciliation and merging of fundamentally opposing principles. This often leads to a kind of spiritual indigestion, a blurring of the line between good and evil, sentient and non-sentient life forms, God and the devil. "It's all one" has become the knee-jerk response to every theological question.

Espoused by New Age intellectuals and un-believing churchmen, this satanic deception has contributed mightily to the decline of the West. Unable or unwilling to grasp what was happening to them, significant numbers of people didn't know *what* to believe anymore. Consequently, they ended up believing in everything—and nothing.

In order for any culture to flourish, religious faith has to trump everything else. Syncretism has been a direct assault on that premise.

I have a warning for all the "one world" space cadets who continue to promote this diabolic con: God is the God of mercy, but He is also the God of justice. It's later than you think.

Dave: Can you give a specific example of the effects of this kind of thinking?

Jack: I once encountered a middle-aged woman who seemed, at first, quite normal. She was in her early 60s, married, and appeared to be financially well off. Among other things, she told me that she and her husband were faithful Catholics, that they never missed Mass, and contributed a lot of money to the church. I just listened.

Then suddenly she began to perseverate, telling me over and over how scrupulously honest she was, even in the smallest details of her life, going back to childhood. With self-justifying bitterness and a rapidly darkening countenance, she then subjected me to an endless, mind-numbing litany of all the people who had ever wronged her.

I felt trapped. After about an hour of this she finally came up for air, telling me that even though she "wasn't perfect" she knew that all her difficulties had indeed been caused by "other people".

Psychologists refer to this as the "helpless victim" archetype, in which a person presents as being perfect in every way, and simply cannot understand why their life is so miserable. Their unhappy condition is always someone else's fault—never theirs. Ever.

As I listened to her, I had the sense that she dwelt in a sort of perpetual darkness, a joyless state of repressed rage and profound depression, from which there seemed to be no exit.

How did this happen, I wondered? What could possibly cause such acute desolation in a human soul? It seemed obvious that she was mentally ill, but was there something else that wasn't so obvious? Were there other contributing factors? I decided to inquire about her spiritual life.

To my surprise, she perked right up. She immediately told me that she was an expert in the art of divination, or fortune telling, and that she was very well known in the psychic world. She had been using tarot cards for over 25 years, she said, and was quite proud of her clientele, which included a number of influential people. She even taught classes on the subject.

I responded to all this by pointing out that both the Bible and the Roman Catholic Church strictly forbid people from engaging in any occult practice.

She informed me that neither she, nor her husband, had ever read the Bible, and that most of her clients were "good Catholics" like herself. "Besides," she said, "how can it be wrong? After all, I'm helping people ... and it's the only thing I enjoy."

I told her that this was a demonic deception and that the devil, who is the father of lies, attempts to make evil appear good, and good appear evil, in all circumstances.

I also suggested that there might be a direct correlation between her unhappy emotional state and her immersion in the occult.

"*Nonsense*," she said. "It's the only thing that gives my life meaning."

At that, I offered to read to her and her husband a number of Bible passages that specifically warn against any involvement in the "dark arts". They agreed to listen.

After reading to them from the Bible I met with them again the following day, and together we watched a video, "The Devil," by the late Fulton Sheen. Bishop Sheen's thoughtful commentary reiterated much of what I had already shared with them, and was well received.

After lunch, I prayed with them and suggested we take a trip to see an old friend of mine, a Catholic priest who is an authority on the subject of evil. They agreed, and I made the arrangements.

During our visit the priest told the woman that her work as a fortune-teller was considered a grievous sin by the Catholic Church, and, if left unrepented, could result in the loss of her eternal soul.

That seemed to get her attention.

After some more discussion she decided to make a sacramental confession, in which she renounced her occult practice. My priest friend granted her conditional absolution, contingent upon her promise to destroy (by fire) all her cards, games, artifacts, books and any other occult paraphernalia in her possession.

He gave her one more injunction: She was to notify her clients that she was no longer in business.

About two weeks later I called to see how she was doing. Had she given up divination and destroyed all her occult trappings, I asked?

"Well, no, I decided to not to," she said. "I called a few clients to discuss the issue, and asked for their opinion. They talked me out of it."

The priest had warned her *specifically* not to do this.

Continuing on, she said her clients told her not to pay any attention to Jack Mitchell or "that stupid priest". They told her we didn't know what we were talking about. One of them was so outraged at the thought of no longer being able to have her cards read that she yelled "I've been a good Catholic all my life, and even went to a Catholic college. No one is going to tell me about *my* religion!"

I couldn't believe it. How could anyone be so deliberately obtuse? I told the woman that both she and her clients were victims of a diabolic deception, and reiterated the priest's warning that her soul was in grave danger.

She arrogantly replied that she didn't care about "all that stuff" because what she was doing made her "feel good" and she was "helping people." Click.

A few days later I was informed of an incident that had taken place in this woman's home on the night before I read to her from the Bible. At about 3 a.m. she had been awakened by a loud shout; someone had called her name. When she opened her eyes she saw the devil himself near the foot of her bed; he just stared at her, and never said a word.

Dave: What an incredible story, Jack. That business about the devil appearing at the foot of her bed—what was that all about?

Jack: It really happened. But why? Here's my take: In all likelihood, Satan had invaded her intellect and will at an early age by means of some emotional trauma. He always tries to access us where we are most vulnerable; in her case it was her damaged psyche.

By the time I met her decades later she was almost completely demonized; almost, but not quite. A small portion of her own will remained; she still had the freedom to choose. This made the devil uneasy, of course. After all, she had been in his service for over 25 years, albeit unconsciously, and he didn't want to lose her now. Apparently he considered me a threat to his investment; so, like an animal marking its territory, he appeared in the middle of the night at the foot of her bed, to remind her of his preeminent place in her life.

"There are in every man, at every hour, two simultaneous postulations, one towards God, the other towards Satan."

—Charles Baudelaire

"And I'll say to myself, 'You have plenty of good things laid up for many years. Take life easy; eat, drink, and be merry.' But God said to him 'You fool! This very night your life will be demanded from you.'"

—Luke 12: 19, 20

"Hell is essentially a state of being which we fashion for ourselves: A state of final separateness from God which is the result not of God's repudiation of man, but of man's repudiation of God, and a repudiation which is eternal precisely because it has become, in itself,

96

immovable. There are analogies in human experience:

The hate which is so blind, so dark, that love only

makes it the more violent; the pride which is so stony

that humility only makes it more scornful; the iner-

tia—last but not least the inertia—which has so taken

possession of the personality that no crisis, no appeal,

no inducement whatsoever, can stir it into activity,

but on the contrary, makes it bury itself the more

deeply in it's immobility.

So with the soul and God; pride can become hardened

into hell, hatred can become hardened into hell, any of

the seven root forms of wrongdoing can harden into

hell, and not least that sloth which is boredom with

divine things, the inertia that cannot be troubled to re-

pent, even though it sees the abyss into which the soul

is falling, because for so long, in little ways perhaps, it

has accustomed itself to refuse whatever might cost it

an effort.

Dave: Given the nature of your work, Jack, have you ever been subjected to attacks from the devil?

Jack: Of course, but most of them have come in the form of ordinary, everyday temptations. However, the beast has become increasingly agitated in recent decades, as the nightly news attests. When the apostle Peter warned us to remain vigilant because "the devil prowls around like a lion, seeking whom he can devour," he wasn't speaking metaphorically.

The following incident occurred thirty years ago, and is a dramatic illustration of demonic rage:

In the fall of 1981 I rented a small cottage near the ocean on Cape Cod. I had always loved the Cape, especially after the noisy summer season had ended.

I was 33 years old and single. My life revolved around manual labor, long distance running, and daily Mass.

One weekend I decided to visit friends in New Hampshire. I had a great time and got back to the Cape that Sunday evening, just as the sun was setting over Nantucket Sound.

To my surprise my friend Jimmy was in the yard, waiting for me. I knew something was up.

He told me he happened to drive by the cottage on Saturday morning and saw an older woman standing outside my front door. Not recognizing her, he pulled in the driveway to see what she wanted. When she turned to face him he was shocked; he knew at once that he was in the presence of primal evil.

Clenching an ice pick, with flecks of spittle on her chin, she glared at him with such feral rage that his blood ran cold.

Then "she" growled in a guttural voice: *"Who is he? I hate the vibes coming from this place! I want to kill him! I want to kill him! Is he a prieesst?"*

With that, she pivoted back, furiously stabbing at my door with the ice pick, trying to break in.

Shaken, Jimmy jumped in his car, found a pay phone, and called the police. They arrived within minutes and hauled her away. Jimmy then contacted my landlord, who came right over to inspect the damaged door. The woman had actually gouged so much wood from around the door handle she almost succeeded in breaking in, just before the police got there.

The next day I learned that this woman had recently been discharged from a mental hospital, and had found lodging in the area near my home. Lucky me. That weekend trip to New Hampshire probably saved me from getting an ice pick stuck in my chest!

By the way, my friend Jimmy, who died a few years ago, was a rugged, seasoned guy; he had worked as a member of the "deck force" on U.S. Navy ships, and then became a semi-pro football player. Jimmy wasn't easily intimidated, but he told me years later that he never forgot that woman with the ice pick.

Dave: I'll bet. Question: Why did she single you out? Why didn't she go after someone else?

Jack: Because the demon possessed, and those who are in the process of becoming possessed, are always uneasy when they're near someone who is consecrated to God. Depending on the circumstances, they may feel compelled to lash out, either verbally or physically. The poor woman who tried to attack me was undoubtedly driven to homicidal fury by the spirit that possessed her.

Keep in mind that demonization and severe mental illness often go hand-in-hand; fellow travelers, so to speak.

That demonic spirit evidently had some preternatural awareness of God's anointing on my life; it wanted to end me, right then and there.

Fortunately, I had just left for New Hampshire. God has His ways, too.

Dave: I think I'll start paying a little closer attention to my neighbors.

Jack: Probably a good idea. An old West Texas cowboy told me years ago: "Trust everyone, Jack, but brand your cattle." Good advice. You just never know who, or what, will be knocking at your door.

Dave: I've really enjoyed this, Jack. Any final thoughts as we wind down today's discussion?

Jack: You might appreciate this story, Dave:

Years ago, my girlfriend at the time and I were in my pick-up truck, driving to Cape Cod in mid-summer. It was a really hot day, and traffic was a bear—bumper-to-bumper.

We were crawling toward the Bourne Bridge when we noticed a dirty black car slowly moving past us on the left, at about 5 miles per hour. The driver was a woman, dressed in black, smoking a cigarette. As she passed us we noticed her two bumper stickers: The one on the driver's side mocked the Mother of God and the other read, "**Sorry I missed you in church, but I was home practicing witchcraft and learning to become a lesbian.**"

My girlfriend and I just looked at each other; we were in no mood for this. I decided to pull alongside the witch's car and sprinkle some holy water on her roof. My girlfriend reacted by saying, "Are you out of your mind, Jack? Now she'll put one of those stupid curses on you!" I told her not to worry, because "He who is in me is greater than he who is in the world." (*I John 4:4*) Besides, I said, "If she puts a curse on me the 'law of the boomerang' will take effect, and the curse will go *BOOM*! right back on her head."

My girlfriend looked at me and rolled her eyes. We slowly moved ahead. Four seconds later we heard a huge *"BOOOM"*! It was the loudest explosion I'd heard since I was in the Marines back in the 60s. Startled, we looked behind us: The witch's car was engulfed in smoke; she was staggering around, dazed and confused, while her car regurgitated green coolant all over the road.

My girlfriend was stunned; she said, "Jack, if I hadn't been here and actually witnessed what just happened I would never have believed it!"

Her shocked reaction to this event was a barometer for much of Western society; for decades the public's perception of evil has been informed, not by the Bible, but by Hollywood screenwriters, producers, and directors. They delight in portraying Christians as superstitious idiots or ineffectual weaklings who are no match for the presence of evil.

This is a satanic liberal lie; believers are not helpless when confronted by the diabolic; Jesus' divine power and protection extends to us, even today:

*"I saw Satan fall like lightning from heaven …
I have given you authority to overcome all the power
of the enemy; nothing will harm you."*
—Luke 10: 18, 19

Remember the story of Elijah? Filled with the Spirit of God, he stood alone against the 850 prophets of Baal and Asheroth—and they were utterly destroyed (*I Kings Chapter 18*).

As smoke disappears in the wind, the modern day prophets of Baal and their followers will also be destroyed; their time is short.

There is only one power: The Lord God of Hosts.

Everything else is just a passing show.

"BE NOT AFRAID"

You shall cross the barren desert, but

You shall not die of thirst,

You shall wander far in safety, though

You do not know the way,

You shall speak your words to foreign men,

and they will understand,

You shall see the face of God, and live.

Be not afraid, I go before you always;

Come follow Me, and I will give you rest.

If you pass through raging waters in the sea,

you shall not drown,

If you walk amid the burning fires,

you shall not be harmed,

If you stand before the power of hell,

and death is at your side,

Know that I am with you through it all.

Be not afraid, I go before you always;

Come follow Me, and I will give you rest.

And blessed are your poor

for the Kingdom shall be theirs,

Blessed are you that weep and mourn

for one day you shall laugh,

And if wicked men insult and hate you all because of

Me, blessed, blessed, are you.

Be not afraid, I go before you always;

Come follow Me, and I will give you rest.

Song lyrics by Bob Dufford, S.J., a Roman Catholic priest

The following prayers are highly recommended:

Prayers
for Deliverance and Protection

† *Taking Authority Prayer* †

Lord Jesus Christ, In Your Name I take authority and I bind up all the powers and forces, in the air, in the water, in the ground, in the underground, in the netherworld and in nature. I claim Your Lordship Jesus over the air and atmosphere. I forbid all demonic interactions, all demonic communications anywhere in our lives and in the lives of those we love. I seal all of us here and all that we are about in the protection of Your Most Precious Blood that was shed for us on the Cross.

Mary, our Mother, we claim your protection over us here; surround us with your mantle of protection and frustrate the evil one's power. St. Michael and our guardian angels come, defend us in battle against

Satan and the powers and forces of darkness. All powers and forces not of Jesus, anywhere in this room, I command you in the Name of Jesus Christ to depart from here and never enter again. We pray this through Christ Jesus our Lord.   Amen.

† *Cutting Free from Generational Sin* †

"Thank you Lord that You will not remember the

iniquities of our forefathers against us."

—Psalm 79:8

In the name of the Lord Jesus Christ, and by the power of God's Holy Word, I take the sword of the Spirit and cut every person free from all generational inherited sins, weaknesses, character defects, personality traits, cellular disorders, genetic disorders, learned negative inner vows and spiritual and psychological ties. I cut all bonds that are not of the Lord, AND PUT HIS CROSS BETWEEN us, our parents, our grandparents, our siblings, our offspring, our mates (and any relationships that our mates have had with others in the past). I cut all bonds of the relationships of each one of us that are not of the Lord back to the beginning of time, and by the sword of the Spirit, and in the name of Jesus Christ, I say that we are cut free, and we are free indeed. We are now free to become the children of God the Lord always intended us to be. In the name of Jesus Christ.   Amen.

† *A Prayer to Break Any Curse*
That May Have Been Placed on You †

Lord Jesus Christ, I believe that You are the Son of God; and the only way to God, and that You died on the cross for my sins, and rose again from the dead.

I give up all my rebellion, and all my sin, and I submit myself to You as my Lord. I confess all my sins before You, and ask for Your forgiveness—especially for any sins that have exposed me to a curse. Release me from the consequences of my ancestors' sins.

By a decision of my will, I forgive all who have harmed me or wronged me—just as I want God to forgive me. In particular, I forgive _____.

I renounce all contact with anything occult or satanic. If I have any "contact" objects, charms, games, artifacts and books, I commit myself to destroy them. I cancel all Satan's claims against me.

Lord Jesus, I believe that on the cross, You took upon Yourself every curse that could ever come upon me. So I ask You now to release me from every curse over my life, in Your name, Lord Jesus Christ! Amen.

† *Anima Christi* †

Soul of Christ, sanctify me. Body of Christ, save me. Blood of Christ, protect me. Water from the side of Christ, wash me. Passion of Christ, strengthen me.

My Lord Jesus, hear me. Within Thy wounds, hide me. Never permit me to be separated from Thee.

From the malignant enemy, defend me.

And at the hour of my death, please call me, and bid me come to Thee, so that with all Thy saints, and all Thy holy angels, I may worship Thee forever and ever. Amen.

Chapter Six

COMING HOME

" … Home is the sailor, home from the sea, and the hunter, home from the hill."
—Robert Louis Stevenson

Dave: So what brought you to New Hampshire, Jack?

Jack: I first came here in 1954. My family had relatives who lived a short distance from Mount Monadnock, near Keene. It became a very special place for me, even as a boy.

Dave: What made it so special? What drew you in?

Jack: I discovered something here that has forever touched my soul; an intense awareness of the sacred in the land itself. From the very beginning I knew that this was holy ground, and that someday I would return.

Dave: A foretaste of heaven, perhaps?

Jack: Perhaps. Ayn Rand suggested that although we've found the music, we have yet to find the words, that the best things can never really be spoken of. She was probably right.

Dave: And yet we keep trying, don't we?

Jack: You bet. I guess that's why we're having this conversation.

Dave: In addition to being a former Marine I read somewhere that you are a Mayflower descendant and a Son of the American Revolution. Is that accurate?

Jack: Yes.

Dave: You're also a Christian conservative.

Jack: Absolutely, which is another reason why I choose to live in New Hampshire.

Dave: Care to elaborate?

Jack: Sure; there are fewer liberals here. For that reason alone I'm much happier in this neck of the woods.

Dave: Ditto. Tell us more.

Jack: Liberalism is a malignant disease, a deadly cancer which has been eating away at the core of our republic for decades. With the exception of New Hampshire, and a few other pockets of resistance, I consider the entire Northeast enemy-occupied territory. On any given day you'll find more committed Marxists in Harvard Square than in Red Square; they don't call it "The Peoples' Republic of Massachusetts" for nothing.

But the good news is that countless Americans are finally waking up; they realize that the mindless embrace of liberal ideology has been a

form of cultural suicide. The terrifying consequences of the first 3 years of the Obama
Administration were enough to get anyone's attention, even the most politically unaware among
us. **Existential fear is a powerful inducement to
rise and shine.**

Dave: You must have been thrilled by the re-
sults of the 2010 mid-term elections. I know I was.

Jack: Most definitely. Conservatives now
have more political representation in the New
Hampshire State House than at any time since
1962, to say nothing of the tremendous gains we
achieved throughout the rest of the country.

We've finally begun to take our country
back from the forces of darkness, from the tyranny
of the left. There's a hard road ahead of us; an

awful lot of destructive nonsense has to be un-done. By the grace of God, we shall prevail.

English philosopher Edmund Burke said: "All that is necessary for the triumph of evil is that good men do nothing." Thankfully, the silent majority finally stood together as one and shouted *"ENOUGH!"*

The solution to our many difficulties is at hand; God is calling upon His people to return to Him. When we as a nation begin to truly repent, and turn back to Him, God will bless America once more, and deliver us from the forces of evil.

"…If my people who are called by my name
humble themselves, and pray and seek my face,
and turn from their wicked ways,
then I will hear from heaven, and will forgive
their sin and heal their land."
—2 Chronicles 7:14

Dave: Jung once remarked, "It is a grievous sin to remain willfully unconscious." From what I know about you, Jack, it seems that the trajectory of your life has been directed toward inspiring people, encouraging them on their journey of awakening. Would you agree?

Jack: Looking back, I'd say yes. My family of origin wanted me to become a doctor, lawyer or Indian chief, but that didn't work out. I did go down a few rabbit trails, but always managed to find my way back. The expression, "God draws straight with crooked lines" certainly applies.

The truth is we're all in the process of "becoming", as Dietrich Bonhoeffer put it. Each of us has to contend with our own wounds, our own incompleteness, our own "stuff".

One of the greatest challenges we face is knowing what to retain, and what to discard, including some of our cherished illusions. Shedding illusions can be painful, especially as we get older, because we are so often defined by them.

Dave: Jack, you've been a spiritual adviser and friend to many over the years. Do you have any final thoughts as we conclude?

Jack: In his classic work, *Man's Search for Meaning*, Viktor Frankl chose to include the following words found on the wall of a Nazi death camp, written by an anonymous prisoner:

"I believe in the sun, even when it's not shining; I believe in love, even when I can't feel it; and I believe in God, even when He is silent."

I've often reflected on the circumstances of that prisoner's last days, and how much faith it took for him, or her, to inscribe that message, as a beacon of hope for those who would surely follow. And here we are, nearly 70 years later, still moved by them.

Dave: That is so true. Thanks, Jack.

Jack, you were speaking a while ago about the beautiful Monadnock Region, and all that it has meant to you over the years. Do you have a special place where you go for prayer and reflection? Hope you don't mind me asking.

Jack: I don't mind. My favorite spot is located about 15 miles from here. There's a river that runs through a wooded area, with a small clearing on one side. From the clearing I can see the nearby covered bridge, built in the late 1700s.

This has been my sanctuary for almost 50 years now, and remains blessedly undisturbed by "progress". Whenever I return, I'm filled with a great peace and the sense that I'm responding to a sacred, unspoken invitation. I'm not inclined to make any sort of noise; there is just a respectful awareness. Total silence.

In due time, I am touched by the Presence, the breathtaking remembrance of Love Itself.

And as I take my leave, I'm filled with gratitude for this holy place, where my soul recollects the glory of the unseen God.

Dave: Home at last, Jack.

Jack: This side of eternity, yes. Home at last.

ABOUT THE AUTHOR

Jack Mitchell, an Orthodox Christian and former U.S. Marine, has traveled extensively, spent some time in a monastery, and studied theology, psychology and world religions.

As a spiritual teacher, writer and public speaker, Jack has spent over 25 years helping people in their struggle for healing, and deliverance from evil. He shares his own remarkable journey and spiritual insights via radio, television and personal appearances.

Jack lives in New Hampshire, near Mount Monadnock.

This is his first book.

10391913R00090

Made in the USA
Charleston, SC
01 December 2011